PLAYING IN WRECKS

Haley's

Athol, Massachusetts

Haley's
488 South Main Street
Athol, MA 01331
haley.antique@verizon.net
800.215.8805

Special thanks to other publishers for allowing Candace Curran to retain rights to her poems previously published elsewhere.

Cover design by Michael Ruocco Graphics.

Cover painting, *Easy Chair*, by Richard Baldwin.

With thanks to Mary-Ann DeVita Palmieri.

Inconsistencies in punctuation from poem to poem reflect the poet's intentions.

International Standard Book Number: 978-1-884540-44-8

Library of Congress Catalogue Number: 2011923600

CONTENTS

I

HISTRIONICS

ORCHESTRATE THUNDERSTORMS

FROM YARD SALE DIRECTORS' CHAIRS

II

MOON-CALF LAUGHS AT A
MUDPUPPY IN THE DOG'S DISH
SWIMMING IN CIRCLES

III

NEW ENGLAND STILL-LIFE

BEST IN SHOW DISAPPEARING

FROM MATINEE SEATS

IV

GHOST RIDING SHOTGUN

RICOCHETS OFF THE REARVIEW

DÉJÀ VU SEASON

ACKNOWLEDGMENTS

ABOUT THE AUTHOR

In all chaos there is a cosmos,
in all disorder a secret order.
—C. G. Jung

No poems can please for long or live
that are written by water drinkers.
—Horace

Histrionics

orchestrate thunderstorms

from yard sale directors' chairs

PIN IT TO THE HEADBOARD

I pull on your fantasy so hard
it comes off in my sign language hands,
a snake skin shining like spider silk in the daybed.

You lift a mason jar and bite the head off a
bitter beer *so carefree* I wonder where it flees,
your pop-up heart when the
high tension wires are cut,
when you go down like the sun spilling whiskey
and leave easy, my madwomen to pick up threads
true or not to weave into tall tales spinning
story after story talking a jag that keeps me
up all night wrapped like a housefly.

My madwomen know
I want to know

Where do you keep your heart?

HISTRIONICS

I walk your apartment
zombie like
over landmines of love notes
historical trinkets
trophies of ghosts lying about half dressed
and I violate
open letters as if they were my own
paper dolls
tender wings yawning
Freudian legs unfolding
cut paste save as

MOON PUPPET

All cicada summer
that last weekend summer
we orchestrated thunderstorms
porch side
from yard sale director's chairs

Your coupled fingers traced
the moon's round face on the rims of
thin glass
whale songs that won her down
from the barn's red cupola
to an orbit we lifted to our lips
to kiss good-bye

ONE MAN'S CEILING

Every night
downstairs
she hears his brass bed slapping
headboard clapping
knocking her off her comfort zone
unsettling her clothing until she
comes undone
broken like the landlord like the
clang-bang pipes
everything fixed to break
all she can take
she pounds fists on his ceiling
pitches a fit of shoes
across the tilting floor

SUDDEN SAX SOLO

BUDDY GUY CONCERT, NORTHAMPTON

Saxophone note blue ice crack
you run amuck cackling
wail yourself free in a high-rise
tell another side of the story
tough on everybody with some kind of
bitch energy
a fight in the kitchen
you get it off your chest
everything been on your mind
you say it all thither and tantrum at a
full tilt crank until
firecracker blue spits itself out
slips down the fire escape slow and easy
tsunami over and once again
you are that conversational sweet thing
returning like ya never left the place
like you're gonna be reasonable now
know how to get along with everybody.

LET THERE BE NO
LITTLE WARS BETWEEN US

Firefly kisser
you say I love you
like a ghost would whisper

you say I want you like a
hit or miss her
ya hold me like
a war resister

get yer act together mister

We love in shifts so
wake up will you
it's your turn

MERCY, BUDDY GUY

Riding the tail
a primitive wail of blue-ball tension
you drive a taut hot rhythm dripping
wet down black spiral hair down
dark marble arms beating against my
arched backbone three rows in
caressing and teasing releasing
pleasing me a layer down

Black and blue angel
your eyes shine a grin of
back door secrets how could I
not let you in
beg fingers to stroke guitar and
string taking me
making me cry for more of you

Hypnotic seducer your pulse
beats slow and sweet inside
freeing with your perfect instrument
filling with your slippery genius your
do me wrong break my heart oh yeah
in a wing ding a
wang dang doodle all night long

BREAK-AWAY COLLAR

Your intimate animal rumble
native to my spine-bending trout-jumping kundalini
arcs bedroom temperatures
aligns chakras
wakes the yearning yawn to dock
to rock and tumble in water and stones
smooth intercourse.

Oh to meet you gnarly dog
a whirligig of high-strung thighs
thumbs up
languid vowels swan-swooning
monsooning
climb a shaky ladder and trumpet that reunion.

Boy, do you see how sincerely
I collar this intimacy
do you feel a snag a bend in the rod
the slow and teasy slack and sleazy
hand-over-fist reel to reach the end of that
tie-me-up-rope Love,
that long leash you say you're on?

MY CAT HAS FEATHERS BUT SHE CAN'T FLY

In my dream I am throwing myself against windows
to wake up
trying to put a stop sign up
In my dream I am breathing someone else's breath
theirs on my face and I'm crazy now
under the ice time is running out
knocking against mirrored glass pushing a frozen
voice out I'm willing to die now to wake up
and finally do to the tortoise shell cat
staring me straight in the face and the man downstairs
singing songs about me that just aren't true

A Boomer's Reckoning

Carson plays toe-tag with road-rage ants,
engages past-life aggressions threatening to
crash and burn her but
damn the hot spots,
she didn't make it to this old for nothin'.

At the last possible minute she ceases acceleration,
facilitating a black hole admission toward some
born-again future progression, the shaky edge of
Ah, is that you Enlightenment?
or a near miss tub spider's death wish,
another clunker vehicle for change.

8 Ball says outlook cloudy,
try back later.

Carson wakes in yesterday's clothes
dogpaddling
in the flow of a bad dream regressing,
up to her neck in the wreckage of mangled sheets
and suddenly spies and wrestles
the keys from her inflatable
woman warrior twin, and it's a
darn good thing because

she knows how to here and now it,
put the fire back in her pocket and flee the
bombastic boomerang bedstead and instead

gather a wake up call,
pool hall break the sky of its marbles and
get herself to work
making it seem heroic,
and not so impossible for the rest of us.

TRIGGER HAPPY

The sayonara poem was loaded
cold steel against my cheek
a bolt a jolt a kick in the teeth
bang click release
chambers empty but you come back
like the movie dead a new release
of re-runs
with me in the part of the bleeding heart
the trigger happy bleeding heart
memory made better in martyred prose
but the bottom line a Russian roulette of the
goodbye sign and steel
cold steel against my channel changing
same thing playing
no sayonara of relief.

ASHES, ASHES

Love is a monster that
swallows whole leaving
not much but compromised
bone when it's done
skeletal refuse the fear and
hysteria played out the
clawing with dust settling
ashes that bless
daddy's visitation rites
a happy meal brought back
so daughter can cartwheel
cutout his heart and
mother can learn
to stay from the windows

"Watch Dad watch.
The next one will be perfect!"

THE FIRST TIME

a blanket under cellar stairs
on a dungeon floor
the furnace firing and your mother
clicking heels on the sky above us

a new geography we were
armless sea creatures on dry land
butting bullying everything sharp as a
blind man's shtick defeat the sharpest

stab of all the first time
we bobbed up with interrogation by
kitchen fluorescence your hide and seek sister
persisting following with emergency sirens

"Where were you?"

CHORDS OF A CURIOUS COURT CASE

She is in plain wrapper budding pink below,
love wish caught deep in the throat, poor bird.
She flutters, flirting with dangerous oxygen,
her pulse pleading in your bed when
in a slip of satin, we are all away.

Her tongue is stiffly hung in its coffin case
and she is strung too tight, dumb girl.
Crimson rises to the top, bobbing up and over
like a joke balloon, trumpeting oh sweet

Jesus! Her voice like nothing bound,
she sings, the way a stone will sing for an
audience of one, bad boy,
whispering harp,
maestro of a bungled blood-song.

A Humbling Slam Incident at the Eric Carle

I'm standing up here trying to slam you with
kindness, tongue in cheek where it belongs but
not where words long to form and impress,
these come from the circular insides of upright
washers and open front clothes dryers,
happens while hands are in dishpans and
dreams are somewhere else . . .
the best words coming in thoughtless minds or mindless
thought hard-pressed through boot-scuffed hearts,
the newly emptied or forgiven and light as sin wafers but
I don't really know . . . I think I lost you at Hello

I'm standing up here trying to what the hell slam you with
good impressions best intentions and words that soothe
or agitate or force a contemplate and of course
smooth talk you into thinking they're slipping easily
off the end of my silver-plated tongue into thinking
the inside of my mind is a vessel, fertile as the bottom of a
washing machine's belly laugh,
a centrifugally forced whirlpool or the psychic healing
waters of a hard to find transcendental dishpan when

gee, I can't even find the cowboy boots I would have
worn here and wanted since I was four for my hard to size up
feet, never mind in the color I could adore and anyway,
suddenly I feel like I have so very little to say . . .
do I have your sympathies yet?

Just because a brain strains poetry doesn't mean
you can get it on paper doesn't mean it can reach

your lips when you need it doesn't mean I could sell it,
hand it over sieved off the top of Alzheimer's head . . .
what was I thinking?

RESPONSE TO THE OPEN FIELD TEST
IN THE ABSENCE OF THE MOTHER SURROGATE

No coming to terms with the picture burned forever,
an infant rhesus monkey
clinging to a mother's terrycloth chest.

Rag idol
guardian without a heart

No coming to terms with the other
picture burned forever
another clutching a wire chest and I remember

discovering about the nature of bonding,
survival and the reluctance on my part
in Psych 101 to learn

how long it takes
to tear heart from its cage.

GAUGE

I got your so called
not a love letter in the mail
and I think I'm going to need some
bed rest
some quiet knock myself out time
to download
reload because of that
attachment clause
that sneaky little love poem
that goddamned break my heart love poem
catching me by the surprise triggering
bang bang blood tears
trails running gunpowder black
causing unstable heart cracks
leading me to wonder
how long are you going to let me be
how long am I going to be
that hard to impossible to
love me me

GOOD GIRLS

He has them blushing and
smiling china doll smiles
old school fool gets to
fondle and kiss must have
missed that workshop
it wasn't meant for him
watched these girls grow up
it's old Bill and he's
harmless
loves the girls and always has
in a circle jerk of them
woman girls
daddy's girls
old Bill in his glory gives
squeezes and hugs
goos and gaws and crows like a
rooster everybody laughing
he has them trussed
blushing pink

A Time Bomb the Therapist Said

In a quiet no show
all show
all masked up for you
cold New England famine family
closet doors are kept closed but
filled with the same old hand-me-down clothes

In a quiet
don't tell
silence falls down an abandoned well
seen and not heard walky-talks the walk
dead guard keys lock the locks with a little
ollie ollie oxen free *do you even believe me?*

Some time in the
near do well
you could time bomb a past life hell
if you don't the therapist said
I think he said
get angry enough

Can She Bake A

Beaten robbed by daddy's love
misplaced
displaced girls can't make it better just a
heart that can't be bartered for a
man that can't be bothered
a bad apple in Billy boys I who couldn't
give a flying what if she can bake
love doesn't take in the kitchen
it's somewhere upstairs
unresponsive
in the drawer with the baby oil
in the brass and iron caught between
black and white lace
a rock and some god-forgotten hard place.

POWER LINE

And she feels him coming oh yes like
afternoon *Jeopardy* like the need to sleep and
she can't put him off because
the ground declares his work boots where
in he comes striking
alarm through the kitchen clock dispatching
terror through the television blushing
turbulence like a fever
shooting through fingers needing to be
wrenched out bitten hard to remind her of
real pain and other things worse than
daddy's home

KITCHEN FIRES

She says she broke her last
rescuer's back
that's the New Deal
and she's on her knees to herself with this one
this hard to hold to promise for no more
inner child abusing
no more plans bent on losing
no more climbing the do you still love me
lap perch
the every man's the daddy search no more
she swears
she chose her last tragedy
not by accident or dumb luck but
good will
her will be done
and she's all done with the old ways
the super hero Band-Aids
this one's coming out into the open
to be cleaned up – sewn up for good
for her own good for a change
and she's long lost paid the cost due for a change
and on her knees she says
she's on her knees with this one

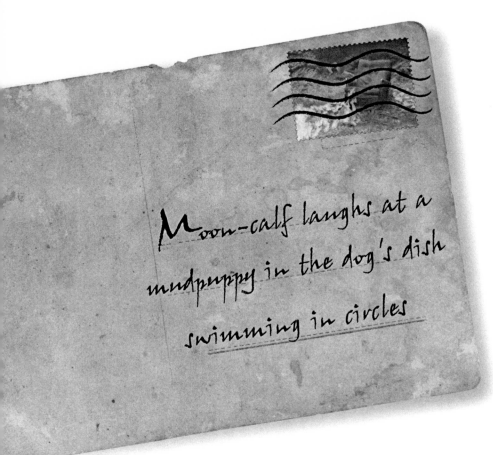

Moon-calf laughs at a
mudpuppy in the dog's dish
swimming in circles

PLAYING IN WRECKS

A tow truck brings in the wrecks
strung up by the neck like shiny fish,
no fight left in them,
and lays them to rest behind Hubbard's Garage

When everything is still life,
the family leaving the thing for dead,
I approach respectfully,
enter and log a sketchy stretch of
playhouse miles

This is where I learn to
Stop Look Listen
Do you believe in ghosts?
Steer, Shift and Look Both Ways
for flashbacks in stains and broken glass

This is where I whisper out loud
a reverent prayer and question,
Am I a crazy child?
and understanding the laws of just-in-case and
you-better-believe-it,
kiss the dashboard, cross my Congregational chest
and guide each soul out of the metal, after me

DOG-WALK DAWN

Suddenly the sun at dog-walk dawn
and even the old puppy stops drinking
Echo Lake
to see morning break,
to hear it take a breath and sing.

Jasper shakes, wakes as if from dream,
the shades gone up.
He walks in to shyly meet
the laughing dog between his feet,
a world turned upside down
between his paws.

LEARNING HOW TO FALL

MOUNTAIN ROAD WHERE THE BARN USED TO BE

Two of us trespass Vickery's barn
and climb the ladder built to the wall
to the tiptop of a hayloft
David Santon and I lift off
to swing from the bulkhead on a long groaning rope
from bottom to peak in a singsong
a hypnotic tick tock
Tarzans above quicksand and hay bale crocodiles

we let go in midair . . .

blood brother and sister
locked together
astronauts in each other's eyes
angels suspended
trespassers catching Time off guard
we carefully count and measure
that hopeful limbo space that
please God place before getting wings

TIGHTROPE

On two legs of a heavy oak gingerbread chair
I hear the hairline crack of Mother's tolerance
her barbed wire commands from the upstairs bedpost
patrolling the home turf
a planting of mines

Downstairs father percolates
scrambles the early morning requesting
four legs on the floor and
I'm almost four and think I understand this
haywire high wire act

Be quiet and alert and stay inside
colorbook lines but gut strings tied to the clock's
sticky hands pull and I
teeter in this tug o' war this
block and tackle need to keep my father home

Eyes tattling shower and shine
but I see through
Crayola black glistening like tar
hear the happy with itself tick tock
boasting when he leaves like clockwork

THE FLYING DREAM AGAIN

Some nights
bright as day I am
flying in the old Princeton Center Schoolyard
my belief in it keeping me up
each soar a pole-vault of hope drifting
gently lifting me over wires and swing sets
trees and the jungle gym each swoop
bringing me closer to the knee-scab ground and
Alan Bobby Carly
laughing screaming
running beneath me
all holding me in their eyes
wishing me up as if I am
their tethered dream

A HARVEST OF YOUTH

Inside the tall summer corn
a company of whiskered soldiers
whispered and *shushed*
whispered and hushed

Within their circle she listened
tried to learn their old songs but became
spooked and ran she had to
fight her way out
flag leaves were blindfolds
rough hands grabbed and snagged with
each path throwing perfect
sketches of the other

How relieved she was
she remembers
to finally stumble from their trenches
and how foolish she felt later
in back-to-school September to discover
the mayhem the regiment reduced
to a lineup of brown stubs
wacky rows with harried mice
traveling through like windup toys

BELONGING

Tides we have forgotten how to chart
haul us spewing
seaward choking
we collect in shadows trying to
ignite new ways
try the fit of new keys in
old doorways
but we still bleed on demand
do what the moon says all the while begging

safe conduct a release a
harmonic conversion
blue muscle and sinewy strand
to form the marionette band
a renegade swarm thick as thieves we are
shapeshifters knitting monogrammed
sweaters the wraparound
seaweed sleeves of sisters all of us
made from the chain of a long
a long line of lunatic daughters

SAY THE MOON GOOD-NIGHT

She smoothes her parent's
night fight
out the bedroom window
pats the moon all right
  it's all right

She untangles trees
bending over crib rails
their shadows hug and climb the walls
for a sleep walk
  jump on

Her mother croons in starts and stops
daddy's patter dots to dots
soft as rain and wax crayons
the stars
the winking blinking stars

UNBELIEVABLE

My mother's labels informed
right up front
cut and dried, stock and barreled,

Sarah Bernhardt
Hypochondriac
What the hell's the matter with you . . .

A close representative of the seen not heard caricature
of my own upbringing is what,
a mooncalf juxtapositioning a cheeky wise-ass
arm up defending threats of soap
hairbrushes, the contact of a good whack is what

and I'm caught in that Zen play of opposites,
a da da's girl on the ceiling hovering,
an out of body projectionist playing, well,
not *Sarah Bernhardt* but . . . Shirley Temple
or her on-screen double

a big show-off whistling, dancing on the furniture,
loved unconditionally, appreciated absolutely,
labeled by her critics, her adult pals as nothing short of
precious and wonderful. The unfairness.
I must have been adopted.

SLEEPWALKING GRANDMA'S BEACH

Sun go down like butter in the water
shiny butter in the water
yellow squash butter in the cobalt blue

Sun melts down black and yellow
tiger butter in the water
velvet stripes of tiger butter
hula-hoops of yellow black and blue

Moon pops up like a bobber in the water
like a mirror sky and water
sea glass diamonds the color of a
glad girl's eyes
beer bottle brown and honeydew
stars like yellow marigolds and fireflies
on bug-light blue

FOR CLAIRE

GIRAFFES

After seeing a photograph of giraffes
caught in flight an impossible
black and white capturing hooves in the air
great bodies askew on stilts tipping. . .
I see them everywhere

On the Daniel Shays Highway
bobbing west on the Orange center strip
two at Hannaford's reaching down like
mechanical cranes
locusts at displays banana green and yellow

At the Quabbin I witness a small herd
whimsical horse-heads that are
masts tilting left to right like Viking
paddle boats making way for sanctuary
puppeteering against purple pyramids

In the evening as if whispered to giraffes
lift effortlessly and I've missed my chance
to ride the velvet silhouettes
I hear them sweet-talking as they vamoose
behind the skirts of sugar moon

CROSSBONES

Me old Mum in the early A.M.
smokes cigars while playing solitaire
holding them in her mouth by way of a
broken tooth and me oh my
I used to think she was a witch
but a pirate she is.

Smoke collects and billows about her
blue heron hair
crawling the ceiling on all fours
looking for a way out.

Me old Mum works crosswords at dawn with a
cauldron of coffee and waits for the paper to drive up
or someone's going to hear about it
crossing the road in a flowing nightgown and cloak
out she goes hell or high water
in anything you could throw at her.

My mother discusses politics with the cat
talks back to the scanner that spits in the corner
of the lookout window where she waves
napkins to startle bully jays at the feeder.

On top of the round world my old Ma
reads the obits and the stars
feeds deer and the occasional grandchild come visiting
to sit on her lap and my oh my
I can remember when she used to yodel and
play the ukulele and I thought *witch*
but now I'd say . . . it's a pirate she is.

38 Ford

WENDELL PASTURE

She learned to drive
in the wide open places of the field
air opening and closing around her as she took
sudden decisions to turn
leaving spaces
outline of truck here and then gone
sky filling the path behind her.

She practiced every chance
brake-foot shaking jaw clenched
back aching
uncertain till the day came when
arm became the extension of shift and
clutch the old meeting place of catch and go.

One night darker than the inside of a cow
she dressed and went out to test her
driving vision.
She made her way along the worn crazy eight
by the feel of the wheel and some kind of
second sight it must have been
Her Grandma that raised her
worried out the upstairs window . . .
Should I get Uncle up
but what she did instead was get herself
a midnight ride and the peace of mind
the conviction the girl's
headin' in the right direction.

FOR ROSEY

43

MAGIC CHILD

She thinks she can will the sun out of its socket,
giant all eye, mighty one, warmth giver of
life and everything.

She still thinks all grown up as she is,
that she can destiny the sun,
draw it out of its dark desires and open it
like a stubborn jar . . . Voila! she will show you
the place to put your two feet solid,
where your face lifted,
gets kissed by that old puppy,
that big old piece a gold she swindles for ya. . .

I remember a girl that used to think
life was a magic show.
She could ascend and fly before love, kindred,
imploded, *that breach*. . .
before she flinched and innocence, balancing on its
last chance dropkicking, went out spinning,
landing her a woman-child,
heavy and still in any man's arms.

There was a girl could sweet-talk the glowering sun
to boardwalk and shine and didn't she,
her glad little heart out.

ATTENDING

As a seeing eye
she traveled past yarn doll smiles
curled and pasted caught ten little
hand dummies flashing red
she saw cowbells at the eyes
read cryptic fatigue a roller piano landscape
shadows cast on a dirty smokescreen

As witness
she collared secrecy
dragging it out to be seen and heard
she heard
sounds aligned to the cicadas whine
a stolen cadence reserved in song
for sad eyed dogs and whipping trees

As exorcist she put ghosts to rest
the magic making kid napping safe
the splitting flock to gather in
she turned lights on in the nursery
made a safe-house of the playhouse
glue-gunning furniture piece by secondhand
second chance peace

FOR J.

SPRING DANCE OF THE SUGAR MAPLES

Fairy tale ladies
In yellow gowns and slippers
Dance from golden strings

Up and down they fly
Sweeping bottom, reaching sky
Delicate wind chimes

The King's bold daughters
Dance through the night, enchanted
Wearing out their shoes

CROWING HENS

He would never
crack the silence with his whistle
it was a mellow industrial
shuffle of air
not an exclamation suddenly spilling
trilling in make-a-scene highs or lows
oh no

Dad's whistle while you work was the
quiet talk to yourself of a man
having learned long ago
the word shaddap.

THE NEW MATH:
CONVERTING MIXED NUMBERS TO FRACTIONS

Mr. Becker made a new seating arrangement
calling names from first to last.
Everyone knew the order,
everyone got it from smartest to not.
The heads of the wounded lolled toward desks
in undeterminable deaths.

His division was a disturbance in our universe,
a surprise attack from an unexpected sniper
displacing the cosmic space
triggering an unbalance of energy
tilting the classroom, laying us flat as a
dodge ball massacre.

It took the wind out of my class-clown sails.

I think he was surprised by the collective pack,
the loyalty we had for each other.
It wasn't lost on him and he tried to win us back
from his own failed grade,
but would carry it through the year like my
C-for-Candace place value.

A Mother's Gift

Empty vessels take shape on the velvet sands of
Grandma's beach. Head down, combing,
Emily has been searching for mine,
measuring for the fit of thumb,
calculating the length of her mother's worry.

My daughter will have me believe
a stone can bear the weight of the world
and fixed complaint tossed to an ocean's
break and spill, unravel to troll
some bottomless sleep.

You're cold, I call down the beach where
each rock beyond the next sirens.
Heart manages its own nest and mine is nestled
in a stronghold, a treasure gone soft
to silk with all the rubbing.

For Em

49

CEMETERY WORKERS REST THEIR SHOVELS

She releases a shower song
from the sill of an open window

to the beat of a hot water heater
in the heat of love snagged in the limbs,

a mongrel language part Wôpanâak
foxglove, fisher cat

the lost epic a dirge a simple rusty
hinge unleashed

bursting the wings of woodpigeons
freezing a gravedigger's shovel

halfway to his mouth

JOY RIDE

Coming home late
mother takes my head in her lap
she wraps wisps of hair around my ear
smoothing soothing
and I let the car heater do the breathing
and I dream in careful stillness hoping
we will never get there
never slow and swing into
the gravel driveway
that spell breaking stop.

RESPONSE

Word-smithy you are no slouchy loser
you are the man that can hold a woman like me
in the deep bowl of his body
make it rise and sing
hold me in some dumb-fucking goodness of
bearpaw and sapling so that
I want to build a tree-house there
garden and spar laugh with you
coydogs under the hunter's tarnished moon
green with envy at we to be
lovers in a firm purchase bearing witness to
scarecrow heartbones thumping
tin-eared but sincere and oh so tender to
that newly made that new old
that bright bird song

FOR W.

SHE THINKS TOO MUCH

She thinks she can take no more but
a sharp rose quartz to her
thin bird throat.
She thinks she could lie down in the forest,
become wood
or hang like heavy leaves in a
cluster of limbs,
one of November's grey

She thinks she could sing
like a whale,
a shrill fiddle string played
rope-tight in thin air,
the last breath, a cobalt
sea of sky

It should be easy, she thinks,
to cut a small hole,
dream stones to rise, escape,
to ease her own heart
up and up bird-like
to settle nowhere

THE ONION PATCH

EAST PRINCETON

I skated out to the black ice
on the frozen Onion Patch

for a Girl Scout skating party
hot chocolate and an airplane circling

and a surprise parachute jumper
the husband of our scout leader

with three of their children
when his chute did not open

and he fell from the sky
in a long exclamation mark

unzipping blue brilliance
from marshmallow clouds

to the place I had been
on my back looking up

arms and legs in the childhood
motion of angels

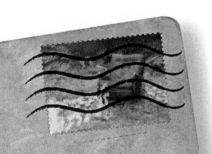

New England still-life

best in show disappearing

from matinee seats

DOWN A QUABBIN GATE

Long ago, farmers planted varieties of
New England fieldstone
like potatoes in long neat rows.

Every now and then I come across them,
naturalized, some growing in clumps
while others wander

aimlessly, distracted without
purpose or direction
leading us astray perhaps

this way, that way
looking like Grandpa's tumbledown teeth
losing hold or the

monuments of kin leaning, pointing,
footing lost somewhere under
the fertile deep.

A Dustpan's Farewell

In a cut-glass vase
the end of day lilies
having had their one electric showing
art exhibition
famous fifteen
close freckled faces like cartoon bananas
old umbrellas
exhale like dog-tired poodle balloons
crawling off
barking their last
drying fading husk and hulls
behind the couch trumpeting last farewells
in this sweet and feckless
reckless world

Good-bye sweet lily bouquet
lilies only get one day
summer's greetings too soon and sadly
unceremoniously
debriefed
decamped
ousted and elbowed out like the
hind wheels of hard luck
are scooped up for a dustpan's fate
chucked for the newly staged
orange tigers corralled in a cage
reinstalled to grandstand
Grandmama's
finely cut glass vase

VISITING CLIFF HOBBS'S FARM

HOBBS ROAD, PRINCETON

He brought them from the barn
humble, but showing off
I could tell
treasure
like children
but better mannered than me,
two golden calves, twins in a wooden
yoke he carved.

In a language of their own
haw and gee
to a tender switch,
the beasts pulled a toy cart
all the time trying to get close,
to nuzzle him,
looking for reward in his pockets
and finding it in rough hands.

When at last we were to leave
they said their prayers,
both on their knees when he asked them to
but thank you,
my only trick,
would not come quick or sure enough
for mother, a disappointed
mistress without praise.

AS WE APPROACH

Spring-wound rabbits run from lily beds
like white-tailed deer.

We sit alongside with a rope-tow of goslings
top heavy, plop-drop planting themselves,
rooting and tickling
interrupting like yakkety-yak children
grabbing dinner from the grass,
pulling at our clothing till we belly laugh
and they laugh too before folding,
falling in slow motion,
chins to feather duster chests.

When sun can no longer hold her face up,
goslings follow obediently to lock-up like
paddle pull-toys.
Across the lawn, poker-faced rabbits play
Red light
Green light
returning to the underskirts of lilies,
turning softly
on and off to stone.

FOR LINDA

LAST FIREMAN'S BALL

ENFIELD, MASSACHUSETTS • APRIL 27, 1938

The building swayed
frail as a paper sack
and laughter and tears bumped elbows
like the neighbors they are and when
reunion took turns
handkerchief eyes shook hands
hello and goodbye in the hollows of arms
in the halo of headlights and stars

every one tender
everyone lovers tonight

PAINTING A NEW ENGLAND FARM TRUCK

MAPLE GROVE FARM, ORANGE

I.
Under the full-blown tied-off moon
dream lighting
milky blue stream-lighting
the icebox ghost truck
staked to the middle of an open field
exhales.

Metallic crows shiver on the flatbed
rattling morning
shaking night off like a dust bath.

Morning reveals outline of truck
landscape of truck organic
feel and memory part of the green
the budding flower.

Barberry pops the hood.

II.
Two draft horses Jack and Jill
feet big as roosters pound the meadow floor
arcing toward the painter until she names them
anointing them sweet and shy.
Over her shoulder Jack steals a banana from her
shirt pocket as she paints a puzzle piece sky
brackish Rorschach skin of truck
black rubber wheels stuck at the wallow
swallowed in pasteurized goose poop green

a quicksand
a slow pastoral a new England still-life
disappearing as fast as the paint dries.

III.
It was Dad's old truck
Learned to drive on her
drove her old bones out
planted her in the field
first love
the keys still in it
belonging to the farm like cow chicken
get-the-hay-in and attached now
as he is to the land
as the family of farmers before.

FOR JOHNNY MOORE

POND LIFE

In an early morning
rip-roaring conversation
wind and sun bomb Frye's Pond with laughter
lifting moon, *old bobber,*
from his portrait on the water.

Black ducks squeezebox
clap and chuckle,
walk the jump-rope wake of water.

Corkscrew pines reflect and *shiver.*
Geese call, one to seek the other
sounding a bit like an orchestra pit
of crazy clarinets.

A TURNING OF ATTENTION

Filling the kettle at the
kitchen sink window
I am witness to cloud-like riders rising
from the backs of black and white cows

Kamikaze crows
fighter pilots jumpstarting are
broken-winged helicopters
flapping pathways to the spruce

Cashmere deer posturing
stand like backyard statues
cardboard practice targets until
I catch one bend and then two more

I am wooing sleep
in the kitchen spooning sleep
my chin on her soft shoulder
resting against heart nesting
dreaming the animals birds
kitchen appliances when

Sun winks at the toaster
a silver explosion of white-light
a God-message meant just for me and
cat who brings me back on her
lamb-blatting mew.

GOLDEN EGGS AT GATE 40

Two mute swans
squatters on Pottapaug Pond
break a mercurial surface
an inaudible siren of stars

We squint for some time
having come a good distance
with only wonder to say

On the way out of old Dana common
we find cobblestone foundations
moss green and old money
nestled in the grasses

FOR MARA

OUTSKIRTS

In the bottom of the bellycave
round and high as a full tit moon
in a halt and suck of night
the bone's horizon falling rising
sleep jerks like ping pong
inside outside I'm hearing
cats screaming love and torture
a motorcycle kicking out a rear
sirens whirling up a distant city heat
all rattle and roar until

the clockwork winds down
and the only sound is squatter crickets
scraping out a beacon in the tightly shaven
blond whiskers of a newly scalped field.

THIEVES

We lift summer from a folksy
Moses calendar
her thick mural rolled out on the dashboard
to play on side mirrors

We make escape through Vermont, New York,
the Hoosatonic's soft pallet
unwinding Grandma's fawn haystacks
like pecan rolls out the back

All the while cicadas whine
high voltage
they try to weld us to an August still life
but we're not having it

From the Bridge over Halfmoon
home to Barton Cove
the early Loosestrife paints a disappearance
scrapping the gold for moonless black

FOR JANET

EATING GRINDERS ON LINDGREN'S BARN

Perched on the spine of the red barn
two old girls fly Evel Knievel
with a swoop of blue-grey swallows
in rollercoaster loop-de-loops
in devil may care dives before settling
at nightfall to their backsides
feet grounded to a checkerboard of
cockeyed shingles

Down below a witness stand of disbelieving
sunset-painted lilies
stretch goosey necks all atremble in
trampoline beds their vermilion sheets
a stadium wave
mahogany faces in a silent roar
patty-cake us
a generous high five

JUMPING ON THE BED

Let me fall onto your
soft October quilt
leap from a mountain ledge
dropping
head over heels falling
into autumn's buff

I want to sink to soft boughs
feel the give and the take
come up once more
and down again like the trampoline spring
of Grandma's feather bed

It would all be in slow motion
a slow savored motion
a color burnt leaf
giving up the tree

CASTING INNOCENCE

Jupiter the barn cat
hop-stalks a Buddha chipmunk
in stonewall prayer.
She holds the secret of October's coming
in the rim of her yellow moons,
under the shine of her butter skin.

Catching me watching
she widens and winks,
setting her eyes,
sinking the sun.

Tonight she will tuck her secrets in
head to tail,
dream creatures fat and still
on stone plates.

GROUNDCOVER

For some of us November is bleak, speechless,
old world mannered,
moth-eaten.
We maneuver it with respect,
walk its gun-crack woods
stiff and cold avoiding eye contact with animals
brought home to tear-drop backyard trees.

Some of us give thanks for
plastic wrapped Butterballs,
someone else's dirty-work and
we eat our way through it,
sleep November like bear,
hope to come out its open O mouth
sporting a new calendar page,
picture perfect,
the plush green of a Christmas tree farm,
splashes of red and blue at the feeder,
a buck laying fresh track,
the snow, the skyline, his breath blowing white.

HUNTING DECORATIVE BERRIES

On an off ramp Route 2
outskirts loop through wilderness
a wannabee industrial cul-de-sac
a scrub pine borderline perkable
no man's yet land
we find blood red berries
sequined sentinels at attention
a double take in a landscape
the color of partridges
pilgrims
paper bags
November

HARNESS

SPRUCE HILL FARM, RUTLAND

Finishing chores, he leaves sweet hay
and large dark eyes in stanchions.
The cold moon waits
outside barn doors.

Parlor lights slant marigold,
panes askew on ice-blue snow,
a beacon to the bellied stove and
cats that keep a furrowed couch.

Like the farmer before,
he shakes off night's dark jumper
pinning it to a hook to rest its shadow
stock-still, as confident of his return
as the trusting cows.

FOR HOWARD DAVIS

CROSS COUNTRY SKIING IN HARVARD FOREST

Fireball sun, you bully,
aiming for the trees you have them
reaching for the sky
gesturing surrender, reluctantly dropping
weapons of ice they play
dead but you don't see

their shadows sprawling
in angles, dark and sultry on the
soft face of four o'clock snow,
grey soldiers crawling away like
spies in the half light
right under your blind eye.

ONCOMING

Wind whistles a jagged rag
scything rusty grasses,
lamenting with her song, a season lost,
the signing of good-bye

Painting whiskey in the afternoon
Autumn casts a twilight spread,
maple reds and turmeric on pumpkin moons,
a vixen's kittens trained in stillness

Pines borderline and prance
long shadows dance, whittled by a melting sun
Swift River's blood stutters, her vertebrae
cold and creaky stiffen

Sanctuary is a warm bed we turn to and from,
where creatures dream fly or slumber
in womb or warren, in snow-white coffins,
waiting to be kissed

STAIN GLASS

Drive us in silence
to horizon's other edge
let argument unravel
the tight-rope loosen like
end of day lace
take us the long way
home to sun's gold nest
let us lay to rest a night of
frail glass stars
their pale light
bending in to us

Ghost riding shotgun

ricochets off the rearview

déjà vu season

DOWNSHIFT

I bring my attention back to the
road the drive the mechanics of steel
and away from your ghost riding shotgun
your face remembered into the rearview
where did you climb on

Memory clicks in and out on the radio dial
chambers fill with trick lyric until
I'm off on a tangent the breakdown
a ditch somewhere going
nowhere with you

I bring myself back
the ride the road the feel of the wheel
waylaid plans for a getaway
at the base of my neck your touch slow at the curve
drops like a serpent

I drive a thin ribbon of road
soft bones and velvet throat where
sun distills butter rum and you don't follow
where I crash dummy into oncoming darkness
knocking like a lover at her yawn and swallow

A DRINK OF WATER BEFORE BED

Shells and stones
take company on the windowsill
collected from Spring's green mountains
and the cyan Summer seas

They reassure and comfort us
as December insists on a coverlet
tucking us under heirloom lace
and a nightlight of moonshine

JIGSAW

I'm beginning to wonder
What you didn't take
What you didn't fake
I know you left a whiskey burn
And false impressions in an easy chair

You are a malingerer
In crazy jig sawn spaces
In empty bullet places
You left a dangerous taste
In a mouth heart-burned

THE HOUSE MERLOT

This merlot makes my lips
fruity and full like the hum of a beehive
and brings out
sex buried
three years maybe
and a desire for music
thumping bold and dirty
lifting me out to drift the tattooed sidewalks
to flirt with overhead stars pulling
chin up to be kissed

Cop cars crawl uncertain
but I don't barter boundary and position
who determines where I belong
judges right or wrong
Rorschach stains
deep within us that darkness playing
its game of tag with light

The central valley fire throws
a glow Chilean red
coaxing dance between blue bruised memory
and a lazy lover's melody
teased to grape stained lips

LANDLORD

He told her
he'd give her
favors
freebies
if she gave him some
sweetness
and knowing what she couldn't afford
she let him pull her
dignity down
like a shade to the floor

Olympic Ice

Sometimes I wake too early with you
sitting on me a monkey
a stone.
It's the opening of September's déjà vu season
and the ice is still so dangerously thin.

The second time I wake I take off your
hat coat
search pockets for weapons
a clue as to why you keep coming back.
You always hated it here the way I hate
hoops rings
the cold snap of fingers
but all I'm able to find
between you me and the cloak's dark lining
is a burning cold
long ago gold.

DUST COVERS

Midmorning
sensible kitchen chairs make me think
you're gone for good but I find
a smile of yours in the bottom of a
raised mug
a whispered message of urgency riding in on
summer curtains. It smells like Grey Flannel
or threat of rain
I listen but I can't . . .

Late afternoon
loneliness plays parlor tricks
hiding puzzle pieces under the rug.
At the sink I recall
what the big picture was supposed to look like
and it begins to come together as I uncover
dripping through cheesecloth . . .

it's me that doesn't belong here

In melodramatics black and white
Memory lays your shadow
monochromatic on pale porcelain where I
wrestle it to the floor

RAILS

Out of a hard dark
in solo pillow talk
flat as pennies on the track
the night train wakes us to each other
stringing from your house to mine
clothesline dream catchers
swinging from November's claws

Together and alone we hang
prayer flags
night gowns
lover's rags in phantom limbs that
used to brag a flame

In the blood stained morning
we are borne
torn from separate berths
worked over memory's knuckled slats
endless cars repeating
across a crooked spine

I Think about Peaches Because . . .

I hear you below moaning like bear like central heating
noises of discontent and misfirings but don't worry—
I'm not going to woo you with my fast talkin'
three merlots and new boldness.
Fact remains that you want me and you don't want me
just a foot up and some kind of relief I can't offer
because . . . you won't take any solace or springtime but
what a tease is springtime, huh?

Your gathered sadness bigger than the moon is heavy
can't be masked with sunglasses
can't be beat with this black and blues blaring
sanding floorboards smooth as scotch.

Oh sweet man and full moon combo
I smell the memory of you soft as peach
but I can't root that stone.

UNDER A BLANKET FROST

On the edge of a complaining chair
he slaps bootlaces
shakes his head against breakfast
and bolts

She chases from the upstairs window
tearing limb from limb
losing him in the fire
of September's fitful trees

In the safety of their bed she gathers
piecemeal
the puzzle of two hearts
and plaits them
one long braid to carry on her back

Tonight they will climb down
hunt the animal that shook them from
summer's easy shell
and she will remind him
show him under silken sheets
the hundred ways they fit

NEGATIVE IMAGINING

On the Deerfield river
between rain and sun rays
shadow and jewel
cornstalks present strawberry blonde

Firecracker colors leak
waves that hint wood smoke and
Nipmuck on the water bank
a kingfisher ejects like a crazy arrow

Her best work
falling out of her hands
a dumping ground archiving ash
October peaks melancholy

GETTING TO KNOW YOU

She loosened his tie his shirt his
better judgment
his tongue became something
surrendered
his throat to her lips
a flag going up

She took him
without resistance he became
her string and bone assistant
their demons flying
high above the two

He took her secrets
from the hollow of her
willow spine
his ear against velvet knowing her
tides collisions his hips moving into
the song she was about to sing

WHERE YOU ARE NOW, LATER

The door swung
back open and out she came
a throw-away
a puppy dog
a chore
not one to take inside,
a whore!
But someday when you
move away,
you'll find bits of her,
dirt pay
a strand of hair at the bathroom
sink, a heartstring strumming
out of sync to make you
ruminate on swinging doors,
puppy dogs,
big hearted whores.

Night-flying with Icarus

You rare occasion
blue moon and splendor
when we come together
orgasmic mind and physical pleasure
colliding
snapping stars
burning small holes in bed-sheets

How you go
tailspin and bone-chip
a bloodletting for surrender tipping
crimson up the arm you slip
stitches you've been working and
no looking back
ride off with your name

How I trail
strangled in entrails
trolling dark waters stars and half lit
jellyfish reflecting the well worn path
a tourist attraction
me in the gene pool calling for
an audience before I leap
best in show
Olympic muscle memory keen to launch
hope for an afterlife but sadly
just another angel falling

DRIVE-BY

I don't see you anymore
in other people's cars or in my own
image breaking

You don't play on white sheets
hung and pegged in rows
the projection snapped in two

Your good dog told me you were
wrought and bone tired all
snowed in white on white

Said you're not going anywhere
I should continue on without you
let sleeping dogs sleep and

Anyway this sinking feeling
bones have double-crossed
there's a double feature lost that's why

This is friendly fire
the last dry cry and seeing you in
other people's places in bedroom

Sheets and pillow cases the last
feature in future and verse and the last
poem after this one after this one

UNFOLDING

He came off his balance
so easily when love passed through
unwrapped heart at the kitchen table
sat with it
hands in prayer around a stone cup

Four days later
he took her out of every mirror
tried to sleep in sheets that
twisted everything around until
unfolding
he fell skyward
over the moon's white back

VISITING HOURS

He enters her apartment
as soon as the car leaves the driveway
opens her refrigerator helping himself
he softens his beard with her
lavender soap
lifting his snake-like throat
black whiskers fleck pink flamingo

He leaves an outline
his spine on her bottom sheet
a print of his bare feet on the rug
she doesn't see
his hands rake lifting
clouds that scatter
the top drawer in disarray

When they pass in the front hall
or the narrow market's aisle
it startles her up her feathers
put to flight
in his sights a clay dove
catapulting
captured in blue eyes

GAME PIECE PRISONER

I know you almost called
this morning
when sky fell to pieces
hot ice breaking
soaking pillow case lace

I know you almost
called this afternoon
when sadness came whittling
a yoke that held me dumb

And again
in night's dark chamber
where the two of us lay wooden
in separate beds knowing
it's best that you don't call

WITNESS RELOCATION

I curl in the back
on the floor of the black
Fairlane 500
attaching myself to the powerful throb.

Father smoothes us flat around
narrow curves, solid ground
keeping us on the move
outsmarting with every turn
the full round moon that chases.

ACKNOWLEDGMENTS

To Family Friends Teachers Ghosts
for your reckless generosity

To the ones that came before
and those that came after
Mother father sister brother
Richard the lost brother
my blue-eyed Grandma and Pearl
Emily and Walt always

Homage and bows to authors mentors
Genie Zieger and Robert Cormier
Janet Rosey Linda Mara Claire and Cathy
for feedback and fodder Dick Baldwin for *Easy Chair* and
crazy conversation Mike Ruocco for time and design and
Marcia Gagliardi for her gift in making it so

Grateful thanks to the editors of the publications in which
some of the poems have appeared in slightly different forms:
Bugaboos , *Harness, Dust Covers, Copper Silhouette, Bone Cages,
Stories From Home, The Greenfield Recorder, Art Space Exhibitions,
Interface, a collaboration of word and image; Three on a Tree, Four on the
Floor, The Family Closet, All small Caps, Worcester Magazine, Mosaic,
Reel Poetry, Paper Jam, Raw NerVZ*

photo by Trish Crapo

Candace R. Curran

ABOUT THE AUTHOR

Candace R. Curran not only writes poetry, she champions it. She is the only adult poet twice named western Massachusetts Poet's Seat laureate. She is founder of *Interface, a collaboration of word and image,* a unique North of Quabbin exhibition of original visual art and poetry created and presented by participants in pairs or more. Since 1992, *Interface* has migrated around the area and involved more than a hundred visual artists and poets in more than ten distinct presentations.

Curran is a frequent featured reader at poetry events. She has orchestrated several workshops for new and seasoned poets of all ages. Her poetry appears in chapbooks and the book *Bone Cages*, all published by Haley's of Athol, Massachusetts. Her poems are also found in periodicals, anthologies, and on the occasional Volvo hood. Follow her work and appearances at http://candacecurran.blogspot.com/.

Text for *Playing in Wrecks* is set in Goudy Old Style (also known simply as Goudy), an old-style classic serif typeface originally created by Frederic W. Goudy for American Type Founders (ATF) in 1915. Suitable for both text and display applications, Goudy Old Style is a graceful, balanced design with eccentricities, including the upward-curved ear on g, the sharply canted hyphen, and the diamond shape of dots of i, j, and points found in period, colon, and exclamation point. The gently curved, rounded serifs of certain glyphs suggest a Venetian influence. Goudy Old Style is among the most legible and readable serif typefaces for use in print applications. Titles for *Playing in Wrecks* are set in Copperplate, a typeface designed by Frederic W. Goudy for American Type Founders (ATF) in 1901. Although termed a "Gothic" (a metonym for sans serif), the face has small glyphic serifs that emphasize the blunt terminus of vertical and horizontal strokes. Goudy's glyphs are reminiscent of stone carving, and the wide horizontal axis is typical of Victorian display types. The result is far cleaner than either and leaves a crisp impression in letterpress or offset printing.

Breinigsville, PA USA
01 April 2011
258941BV00002B/5/P